OVERCOMING YOUR BREAKUP

A Lover's Guide to Resilience

by

Jelina L. Sheppard

1

Dedicated To

Benji, The Blueprint.

David, The Road Map.

and....

"Auntie", for being by my side through the blueprint, the roadmap, and the completion of this guide.

Dedicated To

OVERVIEW

Introduction	6
Step One: Make A Decision	17
Step Two: Feel What You Feel, But Be Honest With Yourself	33
Step Two Afterthought: What Happens If I Skip This Step	41
The Brokenhearted Prayer	55
Step Three: Cut Ties With The Past and Move On	57
Step Four: Live Your Best Life	74
Step Five: Turn Your Pain Into Purpose	87

Introduction

Bystander Girl: "What's wrong with her?"

Bystander Guy: "I don't know but come on. The cafe is going to close any minute."

Bystander Girl: "Wait, we should call for help"….

That's what I heard while passed out in a parking lot of North Carolina A&T State University. I had just left McAlister's where I allowed my three friends to finish another wasted meal of mine that I couldn't stomach. Midterms were now over and I could fall apart if I wanted too… so I guess did.

7

Walking to my car, my eyes were filled with tears and I couldn't hardly see. It was like the sixty percent water mass in my body was slowly exiting through my eyes. It felt like such a long walk. But I knew in my head if I could just get in the car, I could go home to get in the bed and "sleep" the hurt away. Each step got heavier and heavier and to walk became almost impossible. I kept replaying the images in my head of them. *How could he?* There he was on her instagram, in bed laying next to what SHOULD have been my first homicide.

    I didn't know who to take out first. Me, her, or him… maybe both? All of us? I was trying to figure out how I missed it and how what I saw wasn't matching up with what he said. All I could hear was him telling me "how would you feel if we got married? We could move to California…. when I'm done with this, we'll plan a special evening for just us two and talk more about it then".

It was like my two senses, vision and hearing, were at war. I suppose my body went into traumatic shock because steps away from my car, I passed out. My world and "family" falling apart was apparently too much and physically, I fell apart…. or down rather, on the ground. I woke up to find myself in an ambulance surrounded by two people, one of them waving a flashlight in my eyes asking me questions that I couldn't respond to. No one knew where I was because for all my friends had known, I was on my way home to lay down. I had dropped my son off the night before with my parents so no one was expecting me. My voice… I couldn't find it. I tried to speak but all that came was more tears and shallow breaths. I couldn't talk about anything other than the broken heart I had been experiencing for years. So, *what was my name*? Boo Boo the fool. *My age*? Way too young to be dealing with this type of heartbreak. *Is there anyone you can call on my behalf*? Jesus.

It was a slow process for me. I didn't break over night, but once I did, I literally felt my heart give out as I was walking to my car face full of embarrassment and more tears. Now, a lot of revelation happened during the EMS ride. Like a cycle, I would regain consciousness, but still remember the hell I was experiencing, then cry so much that I passed out again and again. Somehow they were able to reach someone on my behalf. They contacted my mom and she called my friends.

Once at the hospital, I remember my friend at the time talking with the nurses who were ready to deem me mentally unstable. I had gone mute and was pulling the IV out of my arm in an attempt to "bleed out"... Truth be told, I was fighting for my sanity in that moment because in your first love, you do give it your mind. You give it your all. In my case, I gave it everything, my body, my first born, my money, my emotions, my dignity, my teenage years, a collection of first times... anything I had to give he took it and gave it away.

There are years of details to how I ended up there, but long story short the breaking point was when I saw the person I had been involved with for years in bed with another girl who turned out to be his girlfriend. But for all I lived, I was his wife. I was fifteen when we met so you can imagine the hold on me he still had at the age of twenty. However, it's not really important the details because this isn't that type of book. It's not a tell all. (All of my exs, you can relax.) In fact, it's not important because that breakup wasn't what prompted me to write this, but that was by far the hardest breakup I have ever encountered. That breakup supports my credibility in navigating you to life and your best life at that.

So let's get started. I personally hate books that give drawn out introductions, but this isn't your typical book. Instead, this is a guide on how to overcome your breakup while becoming the best version of yourself. "BETTER NOT BITTER", is the ultimate goal.

You clearly picked this guide up because you're either contemplating a breakup in your future, in the middle of a breakup, or maybe you have been through a breakup and are interested in learning something that would have made your breakup a little easier. I don't want to focus on the stories of multiple encounters with breakups. I don't want to do or say anything that's going to reinforce your pain. The main goal of this guide is to make overcoming a breakup manageable while cultivating a positive and resilient relationship within yourself.

I created this guide because growing up, I always wanted to know how I was supposed to move on. I would ask people for direction and steps I could take to alleviate the pain and stop me from losing myself. No one had any real advice for me. Their favorite line was "time heals all" and while I do agree, I believe productive time mends all.

With my most destructive relationship, I found myself stuck. I was an emotional wreck and while the relationship started falling apart after three years, it took me two additional years to completely walk away and be free from what was detrimental. Once I was out of the relationship, then my process was able to begin. We ended in 2012 but it wasn't until 2016 where I finally felt healed of that relationship.

However, like most individuals, I entertained relationships immediately after that one so I'm still healing from those relationships on my road to complete recovery as well. The process for my 2012 relationship was only a benchmark. In fact, it's because of my 2015 "breakup", which I refer to as my "blueprint", that this guide was created. I didn't want to be devastated about my friend, who was more than a friend, leaving to accept a new job. So I thought long and hard and developed the steps presented in this guide.

You may be wondering why I'm just now releasing this in 2018, but after the "blueprint" was the late 2016 breakup called the "roadmap". He was the second time I had been in love since my son's father and probably the sixth or seventh situationship. It was because of him, I was able to navigate myself through these steps to assure you, THEY DO WORK!

Now it's going to be **DIFFICULT.** Let me reiterate that one more time, this process will be **DIFFICULT.** There are going to be some days you don't want to pick this guide up let alone be reminded you're living without him or her. However, I promise if you push through your hurt and gain control of your emotions, you will overcome your break up and not find yourself in the same situation again. How do I know? Because you will have discovered something about yourself through this process. You will have reflected on your significant other in a way that will help you identify red flags you won't ignore moving forward.

You will have also dissected and picked apart the remains of your relationship leaving nothing to return to. If you want to overcome your breakup and not be left broken then this is the guide for you. If you are in a fuzzy place where you two aren't together but you're hoping maybe you'll get back together, then the first step of this guide is definitely for you.

While there is no set time frame for overcoming a relationship, I didn't have the guidance of this book that you do now. I was learning as I went through and now that I'm on the other side, it is in my heart to help guide you here as well. Throughout this book, there will be interactive and reflective steps. I encourage you to keep a journal and document everything. Honest and thorough documentation keeps you accountable. As you respond to some of the activities and questions, your honesty, no matter how hurtful and raw, is something that will be stressed throughout this process. The truth shall make you free.

There will also be scripture references that I used to encourage you because I have found there to be healing in God's word. These are the words and affirmations I'd like you to hide in your heart and focus on. It's all about where we're going and who we'd like to be when it's all said and done. You and your heart are my main priority.

Will you trust me and let me navigate you on this journey? (I'm assuming you said yes… either way you bought the book. SMILE.) Thanks in advance. Just think of me as your GPS. I'm getting all of my knowledge about where you're going from God.

Let's begin shall we?

Initial Expectations

1. With the end in mind, what are you expecting to have happen once you've finished this book?

_____
_____
_____
_____
_____
_____
_____
_____
_____
_____

Step One: Make a Decision

"A double minded man is unstable in all his ways"

James 1:8 (KJV)

There's a 90's R&B song that says "I don't really wanna stay, I don't really wanna go, but I really need to know, can we get it together?" While I absolutely love that song, being in that headspace of not knowing if you should move on completely or wait to see if they'll come around is exhausting. Not only is it exhausting, it's time wasted. So should you move on or wait? Unfortunately, no one can make this decision for you but I can tell you "anything you do in life should have purpose" (Dr. Kevin A. Williams). Everything you set out to do should help you become a better individual and your relationships are no exception. I don't know the details of your relationship, situationship, etc. so I can't tell you YES YOU SHOULD MOVE ON AND NEVER LOOK BACK, I can however, offer you some advice that will help you make a decision, benefiting you in the long run.

In the beginning stages of a breakup there is usually a battle between your head and your heart. You don't know whether to stay emotionally and work on the relationship or move forward and let the relationship be. The way you handle the battle between your head and your heart is to be very **objective.** To be objective, is to treat or deal with facts without distortion by personal feelings or prejudices. (Highlight that last statement please). Forget how good they look, how great the sex was, the memory of that "one" time when they made you smile, the length of your relationship, or how much you love them. Yes, I said it. Disregard for a moment how

LONG and how MUCH you've invested and forget what you perceive you feel. To make a firm decision, you want to make a choice based on fact. Facts are concrete and indisputable and it's impossible to be objective when you're emotional. Remember, every relationship you have should have purpose and help you become a better person at the end of the day. Moving forward, I want you to focus on that before investing anything into a new relationship. When we discuss relationships, I'm primarily focusing on intimate ones. However, in regards to relationships of purpose, it is not limited to intimate relationships; but the principle is also applicable to friendships, business partnerships, and family. When it comes to the people you're connected to, "these individuals should help you bring your vision to reality" (Dr. Kevin A. Williams).

Vision in this sense, refers to the plans for your life and relationships. Whatever you see in your head when you think about a particular person, should match the reality of their actions bringing what you envision to fruition. Keeping in mind, your vision should not be based on feeling.

If you're in a relationship and you are going through a bunch of changes mentally regarding staying or leaving, or if you have called it off with someone and are now debating whether to go back or move on, then take a step back from those tears and let's work together to make a decision. If after you answer these objective questions, your decision is to move on, then it's time to get a plan in motion to help you overcome your breakup. Grab a pen. We have a few things we need to address.

Objective Questions:

1. Every relationship should yield a return. **What have you been given in your relationship?** At the end of the day what do you get from your investment? (Yes, your relationship is an investment). After addressing this question, follow up and answer this as well: What do you want or expect in return? Are they willing to give you that?

2. Identify the purpose your mate has in your life. **Are they serving their purpose?** If not, is there evidence that they are progressing toward fulfilling their purpose?

3. **What is your purpose in their life?** "If they don't know what you're supposed to accomplish in their life, they won't know your value" (Dr. Kevin A. Williams). Not only should you be receiving in your relationship but you always want to be on the giving end as well. A relationship is a responsibility and you are responsible for meeting their needs. Follow up with your partner if you don't know what your purpose was in their life. Literally ask them, "what am or was I supposed to do for you in our relationship?"

    Are you fulfilling or did you fulfill your purpose in their life? If you did not, and are still in a relationship, this could leave room for someone else to take your spot. (Just something to think about moving forward with either decision). On the other side, if your partner doesn't know what they need from you or where you fit in their life, they will mishandle you. Remember everything you do should have purpose behind it. Why are you in their life?

4. **Are you putting in what you expect to get out?** Going back to God's word,

A. Galatians 6:7 *"Be not deceived; God is not mocked: for whatsoever a man soweth, that shall he also reap". (KJV)*

B. *Luke 6:38 "Give, and it shall be given unto you; good measure, pressed down, and shaken together, and running over, shall men give into your bosom. For with the same measure that ye mete withal it shall be measured to you again" (KJV)*

C. *Matthew 7:20 "Wherefore by their fruits ye shall know them." (KJV)*

These are all promises from God. The principle of sowing and reaping stands firm. If you discover you are not getting back what you're putting in, then Love, it's time to check the "soil" you're sowing into. Sometimes there is nothing wrong with how you are applying the principle to your life. It could have everything to do with WHERE you're trying to apply this principle. An individual who does not value this principle cannot sow back into you. By the way, that last sentence would be a good statement to highlight.

5. **Are they and the relationship worth the work?** After you have addressed questions one through four, I want you to spend some time evaluating question five. After you've gathered all the information, you need to decide if you're going to stay or go. If you choose to stay, think long and hard about this commitment of question five. Whether you choose to stay or leave, it is a decision you

have to be sure about and are committed to. You should never have a plan and midway through stray away. If you do, you were never committed to begin with.

So I ask again, if you stay, is the person and the relationship worth the work? Hard work doesn't immediately pay off, and when that happens you dry your tears and work harder. Are they worth it? If you say yes, then I support you and your decision. Don't abandon the work and relationship when it gets hard. Stay strong and focused. Counseling could be extremely beneficial in navigating your relationship back to life. If you answered no, then you've made the decision to move forward without your relationship. With anything God takes away from you, He'll give you something better. With that promise in mind, staying committed to your decision should make it worth it.

A.   Job 8:7 "Though thy beginning was small, yet thy latter end should greatly increase." (KJV)

B.   Jeremiah 29:11 "For I know the plans I have for you," declares the Lord, "plans to prosper you and not to harm you, plans to give you hope and a future." (KJV)

Moving forward, as you pray asking God for strength and to ease your pain, meditate on these scriptures. They are to give you comfort and to remind you that working to overcome this thing is not in vain. There is something great to be gained here. Productive time mends all.

30

Step Two: Feel What You Feel, But Be Honest With Yourself

1) "Behold, thou desirest truth in the inward parts: and in the hidden part thou shalt make me to know wisdom." Psalms 51:6 (KJV)

2) "The integrity of the honest keeps them on track." Proverbs 11:3 (MSG)

3) "And ye shall know the truth, and the truth shall make you free." John 8:32 (KJV)

I have this saying I tell everyone when they are challenged with something. "Take your moment and feel what you feel." Throughout this process you have to give yourself the same patience and care you initially gave your ex before they broke your heart. You wouldn't make your lover feel guilty or rush them to get over their feelings about a situation. You would be there for them while they went through their process and you have to allow yourself the same grace. There is absolutely nothing wrong with what you feel.

If you feel sad, be honest with yourself and admit that. Say "okay, today I feel sad". If you are missing them, well Love, that's normal and perfectly okay. Once you have grown accustomed to having something remotely close to what you desire, to be back at square one with nothing at all, will make your flesh want to run back to the familiar. At this point, everything you feel is allowed. No matter what the emotion is, it is okay and acceptable. Take your moment and give yourself time to get all those emotions out, keeping in mind acting on those emotions could bare consequences. Once you have identified how you're feeling, remind yourself you can't stay there. Take your moment and keep moving forward with the plan.

At the beginning of this chapter, I gave you three scriptures for reference. These are thoughts I want you to meditate on and be mindful of as you go through your journey. Being honest with yourself will allow you to gain wisdom in how you move forward. If you're honest and say, "I'm sad today because I miss being held by my ex", being cognizant of that will or should keep you from finding yourself in the arms of another individual just because they can ease the void. More importantly, being honest about how you feel, why you feel that way, and the facts of why the relationship ended, will give you the wisdom to not reach back for the familiar.

Reaching back will only start the painful and unhealthy cycle over again. Remember, you made the decision to move forward so that you can welcome healthier relationships. Don't fall for it. Staying honest will keep you on track with the plan. While we're discussing contacting your ex, I want to take a moment and talk about "closure".

I'll be honest, I have mixed feelings about this. I understand sometimes we need to understand why and how our relationship got to that breakup point, however with my last breakup, I had to be honest and admit I was using closure as an excuse to hold on. I wasn't truly ready to let him go and reaching out for an answer to my whys didn't give me any solidarity about why I should move on. I already understood we weren't working because he didn't want us to, but I kept reaching out because deep down I was hoping he would give me a different conclusion that didn't mean CLOSURE. Closure is defined as a feeling that an emotional or traumatic experience has been resolved; a sense of resolution or conclusion at the END of a work.

When people say "I just want closure. Once I get that I'll be able to move on".... I view that statement as an excuse to hang on a little longer. We don't truly want closure when we say we do. Closure isn't something you want, it's a fact you accept without permission or the support of someone else. Closure is the acceptance that a thing has finally ended. If we're speaking logically, why would we go to our ex to gain closure? Are you going to him or her so they can help you accept that it's over? They've made that plain and clear in their actions. If they aren't responding to your messages, it's clearly done. If you've been to their house and they didn't let you in… Sis… Sir… it's time to move on. If you told them you were done, then be done. You won't find closure in someone else.

Closure is an internal gain and you won't find it outside of yourself. They gave you closure when they said it was over. So, I said all that to say, if you still feel the need for closure and you want to get that from your ex, you're not ready to move on. STOP RIGHT HERE and go back to step one. Do not advance and collect $200.00, just start over. Either you're not committed to the decision to move on or you need to be reminded why you're moving forward to begin with. However, if closure is not an issue for you then let us continue....

Lastly, the truth will make you free. As painful as the truth is, the pain comes with freedom. As you find yourself being honest about your feelings, you will discover some painful information about yourself and your insecurities that will surface. Wait, before you get defensive! We all have insecurities and I'll be transparent with you. With my last breakup, I went through this overcoming process yet again. I was being honest with myself about missing him. As I started digging deep to understand why I felt what I felt, I had the thought, *it wasn't the worse relationship I've ever been in. Maybe that was as good as it was going to get for me.*

Now, in that relationship, he never had time for me. He wasn't serious about wanting to be together. He would do intentional things to hurt me when I unknowingly offended him. He would ignore me when we were talking about things important to me and make sure I saw him ignore me.

HASHTAG, LEFT ON READ, for days at a time. Granted, I couldn't confirm he was entertaining other women, so I had that one ounce of hope left in him. I thought, *he's not cheating [that I know of] so that's a blessing. It could be worse.* Now why on earth would I think I could settle for that kind of treatment? Why would I think that was as good as it was ever going to get for me? I had to have a truth moment and accept that maybe I didn't value myself as much as I could have. I had to be honest and admit that I didn't love myself as much as I should. Once I swallowed that pill, I took the necessary steps to make myself a priority on the love list. That meant when he called, even if I met up so I could hear him out, when I didn't see a change in his actions at the first hint of inconsistency, I cut it off. When he called again, I didn't answer and that hurt me.

I loved that man and to this day, if under different circumstances, I still could. However, his actions showed me, he will never do anything more than hurt me. Whether it was unintentional or intentional, I would only get hurt. Not that he was unable, but he had become committed to my demise due to his desire of self-gratitude. I had to accept that. Maybe he did love me, but it was clear he loved himself more than he loved me. Time after time proved that. It doesn't take long to notice a pattern. So no, I didn't give up on the man I loved, I just started loving me more. I made a promise to always choose me. Choose you and choose long term happiness. Leave your ex alone and move forward.

Step Two Afterthought: WHAT HAPPENS IF I SKIP THIS STEP?

I'm glad you asked! I would always skip this step, which is why I kept finding myself in a repetitive cycle with new bodies. I can understand why you would want to skip this step. I can understand why you would begin this process and in the middle, say forget it and try to undo what you had begun. Here's the thing. Yes, sometimes these feelings and this very important step will be overwhelming but everything you have to gain is beyond worth it. I wanted out of my cycle, so I had to revisit the decision I had made in step one and follow through with the process of step two.

Sweeping pain under the rug was harboring hurt and creating an environment for bitterness to grow. When I did that, I only created a bigger mess in a covered, or in my case, internal environment. Think about it, the rug represents the external us; what people see daily. Sure, the floor itself looks clean. It looks even better with that accent rug thrown over it, but if we move that rug, what do you find under it? A big ol' mess. Old trash and dirt, maybe even negative things growing such as bugs or bitterness that breed other bugs like resentment, anger, temper problems, insanity, etc.

Now think about previous relationships or maybe even the one you need to overcome. When they hurt you, did you take the time to acknowledge how you felt? Did you figure out a healthy plan to not experience it again? Or did you just "shake it off" and learn how to function through your feelings? For me, I was that rug. I looked nice on the outside but internally, I had so much hurt and disappointment from things done throughout the relationship and previous ones before that one. I was dirty on the inside and the bug called bitterness was growing. Bitterness grows in the hidden and dark parts of your heart. Which brings me back to step two, "Feel what you feel but be honest with you".

You're hurt? YOU HAVE EVERY RIGHT TO BE HURT. You're angry? YOU SHOULD BE! You're sad and want to yell, scream, and cry? GO FOR IT! You want to key that man's car or cut that woman's bundles? PRESS PAUSE!!!! Nope. I can't cosign that one, especially not the bundles. You will probably feel like I don't understand because I don't know what all they did to you. Just a heads up, I'm not that kind of individual. However, I don't believe in letting people have too much authority over my feelings. Especially if they took my investment and did wrong by it. They get nothing more from me at that point. That's the mindset you'll have to adapt if you want to be resilient. We can't focus on who made us feel the way we feel because all that does is feed the negative. When you focus on the person behind the hurt, you haven't taken back their power to hurt you again. (That was a good highlighter moment. SMILE).

The way you battle bitterness is by becoming consumed with finding peace and understanding. The key to getting through step two is labeled "Intentional". You don't just wake up one day without having done the work and realize "oh wow, I lost fifteen pounds". While that would be nice, it doesn't happen that way. So why would you think you're going to wake up one day and be over what happened without committing to letting it go? Understanding will come to those who seek it and peace to those that work on it.

"Finally, brethren, whatsoever things are true, whatsoever things are honest, whatsoever things are just, whatsoever things are pure, whatsoever things are lovely, whatsoever

things are of good report; if there be any virtue, and if there be any praise, think on these things.

Those things, which ye have both learned, and received, and heard, and seen in me, do: and the God of peace shall be with you". Philippians 4:8-9 (KJV)

I have referenced many scriptures in this step, and that's intentional. The goal is to not only build you emotionally and physically, but spiritually as well.

"For we do not have a high priest who is unable to empathize with our weaknesses, but we have one who has been tempted in every way, just as we are- yet he did not sin.." Hebrews 4:15 (NIV)

Even if you feel like no one understands, the truth is that someone does. I do too, but just in case you're not convinced, there will always be someone on your side that knows EXACTLY how you feel in your moment. Rest in that. Resting is an intentional act of gaining peace.

Now that you understand what is required of you in this step, let's acknowledge your feelings one more time so you know I really do care. It's okay to be hurt. It's okay to be broken. It's okay to be angry…. hear me loud and clear, IT'S OKAY. In fact, I need you to own it, embrace it, and then when you're ready to feel something better, let it go. The way you let it go? Don't hold it in. Where do you place these feelings when you're ready to let them go? For me, I always write out how I feel, why I feel what I feel, and address what I write to the cause of the feelings. If you're feeling extra bold, give the person who hurt you, what you write and refuse to hold their baggage. BUT ONLY GIVE IT TO THEM, IF YOU DON'T NEED A RESPONSE BACK.

"And ye shall know the truth, and the truth shall make you free." John 8:52 (KJV)

You will know the truth and THEN the truth will make you free. You don't get free from the hurt and negativity by dismissing what you feel or by sweeping it under the rug. You can only be free when you acknowledge (NOT FOCUS ON), what it is you feel. You have to be honest. Now sweetheart, this is not the time to get this sense of pride and join the stupidity of "team no feelings". Feel what you feel… but be honest with yourself. In fact, this needs to become your mantra and new way of living. When things happen that make you feel whatever, let yourself feel it. You don't get joy being afraid of sadness… jumping ahead a little bit, you won't get love being afraid of heartbreak.

"Behold, You desire truth in the inward parts,

And in the hidden part You will make me to know wisdom."

Psalms 51:6 (KJV)

Back to that "hidden part", you know that rug you have on the floor?... the inward part of yourself? Once you've acknowledge what you feel, you can began creating a plan to navigate yourself to something better should the feeling you feel be negative. Know the truth and then you will gain good judgement, intelligence, and experience in moving forward. If you're sad, how do you find joy? If you're angry what needs to happen or what can YOU do to be happy? Remember we aren't focusing on anyone else other than ourselves. That is who we are obligated to when it's all said and done. That closure thing you wanted from him or her, must again come from you. So, in your thought process, don't focus on what someone else should do that will make you happy, the goal is to be happy with or without the presence or "act right" of another soul. You're going to be free from this and when you become free, then you can focus on making resilience apart of your character.

Reflective Practice:

1. What do you feel? (release all of it)

2. Why do you feel it? (you may have to relive it one more time to really release it)

3. What can you do to feel _____? (Insert desired feeling)

4. What does that feeling look or feel like?

The Brokenhearted Prayer

Good Father,

You promised that you're closest when I'm broken.

You also promised that by your stripes, I'm already healed.

Even though I've had to suffer,

you promised in Psalms 71:20, you'd restore my heart and give it new life.

So now I pray a little harder and ask you to do something deeper.

I've released all hurt and have forgiven where forgiveness was needed, but I still feel...

and I'm still affected.

Father God, please remove the residue of what broke me.

Don't let the stains of my sins and others' sins against me affect my growth, future, and heart.

Completely restore me. I don't want to just be healed, I need to be restored.

I want to be clean and free.

Take away the sensory of my past and leave only the hope for a new experience,

In Jesus Name, Amen.

Step 3: Cut Ties With the Past and Move On

1) *"Brothers, I do not consider that I have made it my own. But one thing I do: forgetting what lies behind and straining forward to what lies ahead" Philippians 3:13 (ESV)*

2) *"Remember not the former things, nor consider the things of old. Behold, I am doing a new thing; now it springs forth, do you not perceive it? I will make a way in the wilderness and rivers in the desert." Isaiah 43:18-19 (ESV)*

3) *Jesus said to him, "No one who puts his hand to the plow and looks back is fit for the kingdom of God." Luke 9:62 (ESV)*

Are you ready?

Well I'm not, even as I revise this chapter. I'm not where I was, but I wrote this chapter a few years ago and now I'm taking some of the emotion out of it. As I reread what I wanted to tell my former self, as well as you, I remembered how hard this part was for me. I thought step one and two were difficult but when I tell you what's next, you're probably going to want to curse me out and that's okay. I can take it. I'm dedicated to getting you through this. So here we go....

Once you've made the decision about your relationship and you've begun the process of honesty and feeling what you feel; the next thing you need to do is cut all communication with your past. Yes, I said it, stop talking to them. Get off of their social media page. Stop answering both their and their momma's phone call or text messages. Let that thing DIE. You're probably thinking "I gotta breakup with their momma too?!" Yes Love, you do. Their entire family and their friends too, at least long enough to move on. You are breaking up with all aspects of your past. You know that soul tie you have? We are about to destroy it completely. If your decision was to move on and never look back because you want something greater, then no pieces of you can be left behind. The person that is God-destined to love you will want to love all of you. They deserve a whole and complete you.

Give me your phone because I'll do it for you (not really but I would if I could reach you… this is where we laugh). Block them on social media if you have to (which I totally advise). Unfollow them. Delete the messages, the DMs, their number, the pictures, any reminders you had in your calendar about your relationship history… get rid of it all. There's no better time than now. If you're struggling with this, revisit the plan and decision you made in chapter one. HOLD ON TO THAT.

Maybe this doesn't have to be a permanent thing for you. If one day, once you're over the past and it no longer has any control over you and your emotions, if the other party wants to reconnect and be "cool", if you're ready, feel free. However, until you've reached that point, disconnect. The goal is to not **relive** every memory in regards to your past. Getting to that place where you can remember and not relive is what will help you while you're "feeling what you feel and being honest with you". We want to take a moment to feel what we feel about the person and what we had, but we don't want to STAY in that place. We want to move forward.

Let me share something with you that my spiritual father told me,

"It's hard to move forward because deep down you're still hoping the person you fell in love with is going to resurface... but the truth of the matter, is they never existed. You fell in love with the idea of who they were and now you've been exposed to who they really are"

(Dr. Kevin A. Williams)

This is why you have to stay the course. You have to let go because the fictitious version of him or her will never be who they've shown themselves to be. You fell in love with a dream only to get stuck with what you were never going to escape.... Reality.

Back when my spiritual father and I had our conversation, it broke yet another piece of my heart. It was like *really? I've called myself moving on and it seems like no matter how far I go, he, the Roadmap, still has some level of power to break me.*

The truth was, I hadn't moved on. At that time, I was in the process of overcoming my breakup and then after nine months of no communication or sight, we reconnected. I thought I was strong enough and I wasn't completely. As the weeks went by, even though I knew I didn't have the intentions of getting back together, I found myself looking forward to seeing the roadmap on my social media timeline. I looked forward to him sliding in my DMs or contacting my phone for whatever. I looked forward to the conversation and without any intentions, I found myself yearning to talk to him. I became "fuzzy".

When I say "fuzzy", I mean I was in that place of *maybe he wants to get back together* or *maybe we could try again... time has passed, we've both grown... we're over whatever happened*. Let me help you. STAY AS OBJECTIVE AS POSSIBLE. "When people get fuzzy, they get optimistic" (Dr. Kevin A. Williams). The word fuzzy means difficulty to perceive clearly. Lord knows it happens to the best of us. We spend a lot of time in our relationships in a state of fuzz. Only a select handful are actually sure.

I was still in love or maybe I was still connected to and stuck on what I thought we were and could be. Seventy percent of me was sure we would never be, but that other thirty percent..... was stuck. I wanted the Roadmap back.... I wanted the dream he sold me... I wanted them both. I couldn't move forward with not having them both without having "understanding" replace them.

See, I have this theory. We are all holding on to something and we never truly let go of one thing without being able to hold on to something else... but that's neither here nor there. The understanding or closure I was looking for, I tried to get from the Roadmap. I tried to communicate that I needed it and we talked a couple of times. He didn't really give me anything that made sense though, because it was not what I wanted or needed to hear. It wasn't "I'm sorry, I still love you let's get back together" nor was it "I never loved you, I was lying, I wanted to see other people, I just didn't want you".... it was a bunch of fuzz. It wasn't definitive nor something concrete I could stand on.

Needless to say, what the Roadmap told me kept me optimistic; until I had a real conversation with my spiritual father. He was gentle in giving me the understanding I needed but the truth itself was forceful. I don't know if what my spiritual father told me is the Roadmap's truth but I felt like it was something I could hold on to. It felt like understanding. The Roadmap was never truly my love. He was a fleeting glimpse of hope and not my resting place. He didn't sell me a dream he gave me something to buy into.

"You can't buy something without having the proof you've bought it. If you bought something and didn't get the product, you've made an investment and with that, a knowledgeable man understands you don't always get a return. You bought into the dream but it was never your dream to begin with, it

was theirs... and they have probably and will most likely sell that dream to someone else until they've had enough of "what if" and become ready to build what could be"

(Dr. Kevin A. Williams)

So what could I do? I had nothing. I had no dream. I had no him.

LET'S SWITCH POSITIONS. What do YOU do?

You search diligently for an understanding. You stand on YOUR truth. You did what you could and he or she wasn't where you were supposed to end. You journey forward the best way you know how. You fight for an open mind that will welcome new people. You condition yourself to not look back and rest in knowing what's for you will always find its way to you. That's the promise of God. When in doubt, trust Him.

We've talked about a lot in this chapter and it's short because the only thing you have to do is remove any and everything that will keep you where you are. Only embrace the things that will help you move forward. There's a rule of thumb I live by, give yourself twice the time you two were together when trying to get over them. For example, me and the Roadmap lasted ten months and I stopped at nine months before I reconnected. I realized that I probably should have given it at least twenty months before I allowed us to reconnect on the "we're friends" gimmick.

While the goal is to move forward and embrace new loves, the ultimate objective is to embrace the RIGHT love. God knows where you are, how you're feeling, and the status of your heart. He's not going to send "the one" while you're still trying to get over your ex. So, if you find new people are trying to get your attention and they all seem to have the potential of being the one… RUN. It's a distraction to your purpose. If you meet someone and you're interested but you know you haven't gotten old hurt out of your system, be honest with them and tell that person, "I want to know you and I'm very interested in you but I'm still in the process of healing. Please give me a little bit more time."

Time only scares away the wrong people. The one God has for you will always be for you. You won't miss out when you're following God's instruction. When it's time for the right love, you'll know and if you don't know, it's because it's not the right time. Trust God! You don't want a new love to come in and blind you from what needed to be healed. That will only add more time to your process delaying you from getting to the promise of "the one".

I'll end this step with the last scripture I quoted at the beginning of this chapter.

"Jesus said to him, No one who puts his hand to the plow and looks back is fit for the kingdom of God." Luke 9:62 (ESV)

The same principle applies to your situation. No heart that begins to move forward and looks back on the past or runs back to what is familiar, is fit or ready for the perfect love God has waiting for them. You don't deserve your Boaz or Ruth if you're still clinging to your Judas.

(That's tough and I love you, but hear my heart and how much I want you to have what God has for you.... Follow through!)

Reflective Practice

1. Are you ready to cut all communication with your past relationship? If not, why?

2. By keeping communication with them, what are you gaining? What are you losing?

3. Once you're ready, write down the day and time that you cut all communication.

Step 4: LIVE YOUR BEST LIFE!

"For everything there is a season, a time for every activity under heaven.

So I concluded there is nothing better than to be happy and enjoy ourselves as long as we can. And people should eat and drink and enjoy the fruits of their labor, for these are gifts from God."

Ecclesiastes 3:1, 12-13 (NLT)

Yes I said it. It's time to live. My prayer is that by this time, you're not hindering yourself by abstaining from certain activities just because you feel they may stop your ex from trying to come back. Absolutely not! Live. Go out and do things that make you happy. For example, once the Roadmap and I broke up, I wouldn't write and say certain things on my blog. No matter how truthful and helpful it may have been for others, I didn't want to offend him, so certain things I just didn't say. *What if he wanted to one day get back together*? I didn't want to burn any bridges with some of the topics and my opinions. My writing was always an issue for us. Looking back on that, I disagree with the choice I made. Another decision I regret was being the individual who sat home not enjoying time out with friends. I was so busy thinking *what if he sees me out having a good time and thinks I'm over him? What if that hurts him? What if he sees me in this picture with a male friend and thinks I'm dating him? I don't want him to think I don't want to get back together.* I was so consumed with how he was handling the breakup he caused, when I should have been concerned with how I was handling the heart he'd broken.

The truth was, I wasn't dating and haven't dated anyone since the Roadmap. I did however, realize that the person I wanted to invest my time, emotions, money, and anything else in, was myself. Once you reach this step, for a minimum of six months, I advise that you only date yourself. After a break up and after you've started the healing process, there is an adjustment period. You're having to adjust to being single again. You have to train yourself to maneuver and think differently. No more going out to the grocery store trying to think of what you can cook for *bae*. Instead, your mindset needs to shift into "I" mode. What do *I* want to eat tonight? What do *I* want to do after work? Where do *I* want to go this weekend? It's all about you again. I advise you to embrace it.

Regardless of how many people come and go in our lives, whenever we get moments to focus solely on ourselves, we should make the most of it and in a way, be thankful. Self-productivity is amazing and leaves you feeling satisfied.

Why? Because you're intentional about giving yourself what you want and need. I'm never too bent out of shape when people can't do what I need them to do for me. Granted, I might be disappointed when they can't deliver but at no time do I stop progressing because someone let me down or neglected me. I will always make sure I am taken care of. (Proclaim that affirmation one more time). If no one pays for me to get my nails done, I'll pay for it myself. If no one tells me "hey, you're pretty smart", I'll do something that requires me to figure it out and when I accomplish it, I'll remind myself "hey girl, you really *are* smart!". If no one loves on me the way I feel I need to be loved, I'll do what's necessary to feel what I want to feel within myself. I will also count my blessings and focus on how Jesus loves me.

    Quick rant, that's the quickest way to defeat those pity party moments that will try to sneak up on you throughout this process. There will be times when you may feel like no one loves you and if you're not careful, you may slip into an internal depression. When you find yourself feeling that way or thinking those thoughts, QUICKLY shift your thoughts to what God has done for you. In fact, there's nothing wrong with asking Him to remind you of His love and affection for you. He's a good father.

Okay, let's go back to living. Be intentional about doing things that make you happy. Even when you feel like you're too tired, if you made the commitment to take yourself to that new art gallery next week, follow through. You wouldn't expect your partner to cancel because he or she is tired. You have to set that same standard within yourself so you won't settle for anything less than what you deserve.

After you've taken your moment to yourself, make time to hang out with your friends, the ones that are sensitive to what you feel and are patient. You may have moments where you feel the need to rant on and on about what happened and how you're feeling in your moment. When this happens, you're going to need someone that will listen to you but after you're done, encourage you to keep moving forward. Someone that will always try to help you see the bright side of everything you just released. This friend should be your accountability partner while you're on this journey to recovery and resilience. Be around people that will GENTLY remind you that you want to embrace peace and focus on the future.

    Next, experience something new. I don't mean a new person to be romantically involved with, but literally try something new. After a bad experience, all you really want is something fresh, something positive, and something that is GOOD. You want to be reminded good vibes, good things, good memories, and good people still exist. You'll need something good to counteract or balance out the bad. So go after that promotion, focus on accomplishing a personal goal, or clean out and rearrange your closet. (That always makes me feel accomplished). Go to that new restaurant and try a new dish.

If you're like me, you will sometimes feel empty when you're solely focused on self-productivity. If it's in your nature to give, it's in your nature to be a blessing and make those around you happy. I've always found that doing something nice for other people helps take my mind off what I'm going through. How strong you truly have to be to serve others when you're broken. Serving others during your low moments will not only reinforce high self-esteem, but will also allow you to grow stronger. After a bad breakup, your value will be attacked. The way you defeat that attack is by doing something that reminds you of how valuable you are. "If I wasn't here, that old lady wouldn't have been able to carry all those groceries to her car". "If I didn't fix the copy machine after Jamie jacked it up, the office wouldn't have been able to make copies and send out those invoices".

It doesn't have to be anything major like becoming president of the United States, but even the smallest things have value. Do things that make you feel important. In reference to "new experiences", do things that you've never done. Do that thing you always wanted to try in your relationship that you never got to do. For me, one day I'll go on a hot air balloon ride or visit Greece. Travel to that country, visit a vineyard, go horseback riding, try kickboxing, just DO SOMETHING NEW! Do something that will satisfy your desire of wanting to experience a new thing. Live your best life.

Next Steps:

1. Within the next three months, commit to trying at least three new activities or experiences. **What are the new experiences you're going to try**?

2. Set aside time biweekly for you to have "Me Time" where you do something or spend time alone. During this time, you should learn something new about yourself. Once you uncover new pieces of yourself, write them down. **What new things have you learned about yourself that you didn't know before**?

3. **What do you want to see happen for and in your life**? With this question, do not include things you want that require or focus on other people. Only write the things that focus on you and require action on your behalf.

Step 5. Turn Your Pain into Purpose

"But the God of all grace, who hath called us unto His eternal glory by Christ Jesus, after that ye have suffered a while, make you perfect, stablish, strengthen, settle you."

1 Peter 5:10 (KJV)

Months or possibly years will have passed and you're in a place of living your best life. What are you going to do with your past experience? Surely you didn't go through your experience just to say you had the experience. Don't forget what happened. Be careful because that last statement is not to be confused with unforgiveness. You must ALWAYS forgive and release the pain, but when you've gotten your control back, you'll be able to remember and not relive. Don't hold on to what they did or what happened. Approach the experience with the mindset of "what can I do to avoid that situation moving forward?" "What did I learn?" Even if you decided to stay in a relationship or if you two got back together, it is important to always analyze past mistakes with the mindset of how do I not get here again?

If you've moved on from a past relationship, perhaps you've learned what to look for in a partner or maybe you learned not to settle in certain areas. If you practice premarital sex, possibly you've discovered new principles and standards your partner must meet before creating that soul tie. **Let me just throw this disclaimer out: WAIT TO HAVE SEX UNTIL AFTER YOU'RE MARRIED. Fornication is a sin.**

Okay, just had to clear that up so you guys won't think, J. Sheppard is okay with premarital sex. Absolutely not! But

I've been there and I understand how hard it is to let it go and I also understand the mindset that approves it. I just pray God transforms and establishes the renewal of your mind moving forward as he did for me. Let's revisit the idea of "principles". Principles are set to protect you. You may need to update or establish your principles before jumping into a new relationship. EVERY area of your life should be founded on and governed by principles. Before I move on, I want to expound on principles so you'll have a guide to establishing your own.

The word principle comes from the Greek word "Stoicheion" and it's defined as **any first thing, from which the others belonging to some series or composite whole, take their rise.** An additional source defines principle as a fundamental truth or proposition that serves as the foundation for a system of belief or behavior or for a chain of reasoning. So for example, when going into a relationship some of my principles are made clear from the beginning. FIRST OF ALL, I'm not having sex until I'm married. From there flows the other things I shouldn't do such as, oral sex, sex using fingers or anything involving the use of his or my genital area. That's one of my principles. Truthfully speaking, I didn't stop fornicating because it was a sin. I wish I could say that's why I don't have sex but it's not. I stopped having sex because I was tired of being hurt after giving a man something I valued and thought was special. I now understand WHY fornicating is something God doesn't want us to do. It's not that He doesn't want us to have sex and enjoy it, it's because he knows the pain and devaluation that can come from being involved with someone that hasn't made a commitment to Him regarding you, his precious creation. I understand why it's a principle He gave us in the Ten Commandments.

Another principle could start like this, "FIRST OF ALL, I'm not allowing you to sleep over or in my bed". What happens if they don't work out and you have to move on? Remember step 3, disconnect? You gotta throw the whole bed away because it contains memories of how you two cuddled and possibly had sex. This means you're reliving what was probably a good moment and you might decide to reach out in the late night hour. Doing so will undo all of the work you've invested from steps one and two. Now, if you have money like that, do you! However for me, it's expensive buying a new bed, with new mattresses, and a new comforter etc. No one has time for that. It's easier if you don't entertain people in your place of peace. Don't give any room for distractions to disrupt your places of solitude. These are a few examples of my principles that I have in regards to relationships. I have more but I won't bombard you because it's a lot of them. You should take the time to really think about what principles are needed to protect you and your heart as you enter new relationships.

Now shifting back to gaining something from your experience, you should have the mindset of *what can I learn from this?* The lesson could have been as deep as not avoiding red flags or as simple as not all relationships end in bad blood. Sometimes you grow in two different directions forcing you to grow apart. While it's all love, no matter how nice that shoe looks, if you're an eight, even with that little open toe room, a seven will never fit. It is what it is, not everything is meant to last forever. I love this quote and I stand wholeheartedly on it, "some loves and relationships are made to exist and not to happen" (J. Sheppard).

For example, the Blueprint and I entertained each other, the relationship and connection was there, but we didn't get the chance to be documented in the book of commitment. Another example, currently there is tension between him and I with our friendship, but we aren't going to physically fight about it. Or yes, he and I have real chemistry and an intense attraction, but we aren't having sex. What existed in our minds and possibly our conversations, isn't happening in our reality. The chemistry is there, but the commitment isn't happening. Maybe you dated someone and that was your boyfriend or girlfriend (best case scenario), but when it's all said and done, you will only recognize and focus on the love that lasted.

While I'm thinking about the Blueprint, he got that title because every step you've taken while reading this guide was inspired through my "breakup" with him. We weren't in a committed relationship which is why I quoted breakup, but he *was* very much my friend... that was more than a friend. When he left for an opportunity to better his life, I was extremely supportive and understanding. I was also very crushed on the inside. If you've ever had a friend, that was more than a friend, you understand the unspoken feelings you can have for them. When he told me he was leaving, I didn't want to let myself feel what I knew I would feel with any typical breakup. So, I created the steps in this book based on what I felt was needed to help me let him go. That's what I mean when I say, what are you going to do with your experience? What have you learned? By all means, don't write a book. I'm not sure if I can handle the competition, but take your pain and make it productive. No heartbreak you experience should be without purpose. There is something to be gained and you have to discover what that gain is for you. The Blueprint wasn't the fulfillment, but he was THE idea for *Overcoming Your Breakup: The Lover's Guide to Resilience.*

  Despite where we are as friends now and the disconnected state we've put ourselves in, I'm thankful for our experience. Without the Blueprint, the framework wouldn't have been established. I wouldn't have met the Roadmap shortly after him leaving, and I wouldn't have found my way to finishing this book. It's amazing how things come together once you look back on how much you've grown. From 2015 until now, I realize the time it took me to complete this project was needed and God destined.

I think you should know there is nothing extra or special you can do to speed up what's coming to you. In God's time, everything He has predestined for you will find you. I don't have many words for this final piece. However, in the meantime while you're waiting, follow God's principles and live by His word. This means you may want to buy a bible if you're not already familiar and in a relationship with Him so you'll know what His word says.

If you can master a relationship with God and yourself, every relationship to follow will be a piece of cake. While you're in this process of overcoming your breakup and waiting on God to send what's right, stay productive and capitalize on the wait. Make your victories in overcoming, worth it.

Final Reflection:

1. What are some things you've learned from this breakup?

2. Have you identified the purpose of your experience? If so, what was the purpose?

3. What are the principles you are creating for your life and relationships moving forward?

4. Please feel free to visit withloveJsheppard.com/contact and share with me your thoughts on this guide and how it helped you.

www.ingramcontent.com/pod-product-compliance
Lightning Source LLC
Chambersburg PA
CBHW050656160426
43194CB00010B/1960